The Art of Minimalism

Four Strategies To Simplify Your Life Just As
Much As You Want –
Find Joy In What You Have

By Zoe McKey
Communication Coach and
Social Development Trainer

zoemckey@gmail.com
www.zoemckey.com

Copyright © 2018 by Zoe McKey. All rights reserved.

No part of this publication may be reproduced, stored in a retrieval system, or transmitted in any form or by any means, electronic, mechanical, photocopying, recording, scanning or otherwise, except as permitted under Section 107 or 108 of the 1976 United States Copyright Act, without the prior written permission of the author.

Limit of Liability/ Disclaimer of Warranty: The author makes no representations or warranties with respect to the accuracy or completeness of the contents of this work and specifically disclaims all warranties, including without limitation warranties of fitness for a particular purpose. No warranty may be created or extended by sales or promotional materials. The advice and recipes contained herein may not be suitable for everyone. This work is sold with the understanding that the author is not engaged in rendering medical, legal or other professional advice or services. If professional assistance is required, the services of a competent professional person should be sought. The author shall not be liable for damages arising herefrom. The fact that an individual, organization of website is referred to in this work as a citation and/or potential source of further information does not mean that the author endorses the information the individual, organization to website may provide or recommendations they/it may make. Further, readers should be aware that Internet websites listed in this work might have changed or disappeared between when this work was written and when it is read.

For general information on the products and services or to obtain technical support, please contact the author.

Thank you for choosing my book! I would like to show my appreciation for the trust you put in me with these **FREE GIFTS**!

For more information visit
www.zoemckey.com

The checklist talks about *5 key elements of building self-confidence* and contains extra actionable worksheets with practice exercises for deeper learning.

Learn how to:

- Solve 80% of you self-esteem issues with one simple change
- Keep your confidence permanent without falling back to self-doubt
- Not fall into the trap of promising words
- Overcome anxiety
- Be confident among other people

The cheat sheet teaches you three key daily routine techniques to become more productive, have less stress in your life, and be more well-balanced. It also has a step-by-step sample sheet that you can fill in with your daily routines.

Discover how to:
- Overcome procrastination following 8 simple steps
- Become more organized
- Design your yearly, monthly, weekly and daily tasks in the most productive way
- 3 easy tricks to level up your mornings

Table of Contents

Introduction 13

The Purpose of This Book 29

Chapter 1: The Japanese Way of Decluttering 33
    The KonMari Method 52
    The Wabi-sabi Method 77

Chapter 2: The Nordic Way of Organized Living 97
    What is Lagom, and How Can You Use it to Improve Your Life? 102
    How to Improve Your Everyday Life with Hygge 120

Become the Master of Your Space 139

Reference 147

Endnotes 151

INTRODUCTION

I grew up with my grandparents in a little village in Romania. The village had no more than 500 inhabitants, and the average age was also close to this number. My earliest memories date back to 1991, just a couple of years after the collapse of communism.

Thinking back, it was a simple and natural life, although back then it seemed very complex and diverse. Everybody had their role in the village community. We had the herdsman, Misha, who took the cows and goats out to the field in the morning and back in the evening. He just led them through the main street, and all the animals knew which corner and which alley they should take to get home. When the cows appeared on the horizon in the evening, I knew it was time to go home. They were my alarm clock. If I ever arrived home after the cows, my grandmother would see me to the cellar and make me kneel on corn grains. This was her ultimate punishment.

We had the herald, Jani, whose task was to collect information around the village during the day, and every day precisely at noon, he went to the main square with a drum to share the most important news with the people who gathered there. I still remember the rhythm he played on his drum before screaming as loud as he could. Since in most cases nothing extraordinary happened, the news mostly sounded like: "Announcement shall be made that Mrs. Weiss' orange tabby disappeared before dawn. Whoever finds and returns the animal safely to Mrs. Weiss shall be rewarded with a week's worth of fresh milk delivery!"

We had some Romani inhabitants — the men were hired to help with the gardening and tilth while the women got jobs around the household. There were teachers (like my grandparents), shop owners, a bar owner, the village doctor, and a police officer. We also had a blacksmith, baker, seamstress, shoemaker and other antiquated professionals. Clothes and shoes were not sold in the village, and since the train station was literally taken away piece by piece by the poor people of the area, there was not much access to cities for those who didn't owe a car.

The village had a mill and people grew crops and sugarcane on the fields, so they exchanged these goods between them, giving the miller a quota for the grinding. People cultivated fruits and vegetables in their households' gardens, and almost everybody had chickens, a cow, pigs, and some horses. It wasn't a pastime; it was necessary in order to survive the hostile rationing system of communism. People had a weekly quota of an incredibly small portion of flour, milk, salt, and sugar. This caused famine in bigger cities, since they didn't have access to gardening goods and animal husbandry.

The shops were almost empty for the first few years after communism collapsed. There was oil, cocoa powder, some cooking necessities, a weird cooked chocolate called "baton," and a salty puffed wheat called "pufulet." Oh, and in summertime, we had some ice cream, but only vanilla and chocolate. That was it. No one had a lot of money, but even if they had, there was nothing in the shops they could have spent it on.

I'm not talking about the 1700s, okay? This was the rural Romanian reality in the 1990s. These conditions determined my first few years of childhood. To you, it may seem poor and boring, but to me, it was a great adventure. The fresh jam my grandmother made, the amazing chicken paprikash every Sunday, the ripe apples taken from the tree, the tremendous fun washing the carpets with the Romani in the summertime, singing songs and treading off the water from it in rhythm — they are all fantastic memories. I feel truly blessed to have had such a childhood.

Today, we live in the age of consumerism. It is the age of Black Friday, H&M, and fast food. Everything is on high speed. Lucky, I got used to it gradually, because if a time machine took me from 1991 Romania to 2017 USA, I'd probably die of shock in less than three minutes while almost being hit by a Tesla that predicted the crash before it happened.

To be fair, my grandparents' village also developed a lot. There are 10 buses daily that connect the village to major cities. Also, there are concrete roads instead of the good old puddle-covered dirt roads that were so fun to play in. The village has a mini-mall on the outskirts and organizes big annual events, attracting some tourists. And everyone has at least one pair of Nikes.

Certainly, most of us have more access to things than before, but are we happier? While searching for the answer to this question, I discovered the following:

"Compared with their grandparents, today's young adults have grown up with much more affluence, slightly less happiness and much greater risk of depression and assorted social pathology," says psychologist David G. Myers in an article which appeared in *American Psychologist* (Vol. 55, No. 1), and in an article published by the American Psychology Association. "Our becoming much better off over the last four decades has not been accompanied by one iota of increased subjective well-being."[i]

According to reports regarding consumption in 2004, people in the US own twice as many cars per person, eat out twice as many times, and possess much more luxury goods than in 1957, but happiness and satisfaction have decreased.

Why?

Because consumption today isn't simply about buying the things you need and a few things that you don't need, but like. It is about buying for the sake of buying. People try to define themselves through the things they buy. They think consumption excess gives them status, respect, and ultimately, emotional bonding. Research by psychologist Marsha Richins, PhD, proves that people have unrealistic expectations of what objects can do for them. "They think that having these things is going to change their lives," Richins says. In her study, a father thought that owning a swimming pool would improve his relationship with his daughter.[ii]

The American Psychology Association released a study that wanted to find out whether more money equaled more happiness. In November 2003, *Psychological Science* released the results of a research project by psychologists Carol Nickerson of the University of Illinois at Urbana-Champaign, Norbert Schwarz of the University of Michigan, Diener, and Daniel Kahnemann of Princeton University. They examined the life paths of approximately 12,000 people over 19 years, all of whom had attended elite colleges and universities in the 1970s. They were asked to describe how much value materialism and physical goods meant to them.

20 years later, those whose values were primarily based on materialism reported lower happiness and satisfaction levels than those who had non-materialistic values. However, the study also concluded that when the income of those who valued materialism started to grow, their life satisfaction also improved.[iii]

So, can money buy happiness after all? We have this saying in Romania: "Money doesn't buy happiness, but it's good to have it." It certainly gives people peace of mind if their biggest anxiety is paying next month's gas bill.

The American Psychologist Association shares another study that aims to prove that consumption-related unhappiness happens when someone has conflicting values. James E. Burroughs, assistant professor of commerce at the University of Virginia's McIntire School of Commerce and the University of Wisconsin's Rindfleisch, concluded that people experience the greatest stress when their materialistic goals and wishes conflict with their social and emotional values. The higher materialistic and social ambitions someone has at the same time, the unhappier they will be.

Interestingly, those who have low materialistic and high social values, or low social and high materialistic values, and those who have low expectations in both areas reported similar signs of unhappiness than those who had high value expectations in both areas, but they had lower levels of stress.

Burroughs' research concluded that the differences in life satisfaction between more and less materialistic people are not that extreme. "Material things are neither bad nor good," Burroughs says. "It is the role and status they are accorded in one's life that can be problematic."

As Captain Jack Sparrow wisely said in *The Pirates of the Caribbean*, "The problem is not the problem. Your attitude to the problem is the problem." In the context of consumerism and materialism, the problem is people's emotional and financial insecurity. This insecurity is enhanced by the media.

Have a bigger car and greener lawn than the Joneses. Be thinner; Victoria's Secret angels are the ultimate shape to get into. And by the way, if you don't look like Hugh Jackman, don't expect a Victoria's Secret angel. New fashion is cool, having new clothes at each party is cool, eating or working out at hype places and posting it to Instagram is cool. Be as funny as a stand-up comedian. Be as smart, innovative, and rich as Elon Musk. Or better yet, be handsome, super-rich, mysterious, save the world, and act like Batman. Oh, wait. He's not real.

We have an idol for everything — if don't, we create a fictional character and worship that. Commercials make us feel inadequate, small, and unhappy if we don't reach these ideals. But they never cease to share the perfect product that will "help" us reach the idolized status. Therefore, we buy into the idea, and the product as well.

The glory and happiness we experiencing by purchasing these gadgets often doesn't last past getting home from the store. Then when the delirium of shopping disappears, we notice that we're still not angels in our Victoria's Secret underwear, or we're not Hugh Jackman just because we bought a protein shake. And we certainly didn't become cooler because we ate at El Celler de Can Roca in 2015 (the world's best restaurant in Girona, Spain). In 2016, Osteria Francescana in Modena, Italy won the best restaurant prize, so it would be cooler to eat there.

There is always a bigger car, a fancier restaurant, more fashionable clothing, and a newer phone. Possessions don't translate into character. In the race with the Joneses, we fill our house with useless, unnecessary items. We spend our money recklessly to obtain "things we don't want to impress people we don't like."

There is nothing wrong with being materialistic and appreciating the purchase of things. However, it is indisputable that if these urges root in insecurities and their purpose is to complete what people think they lack, consumption won't bring happiness.

Things are much more accessible today than ever before. You can buy a new t-shirt for as little as three dollars for every party, or every day, if you wish. My dad used to buy three shirts a year when he was younger — a white, a black, and a blue one. There was not such an abundance of shirts on the market. They were not cheap, but they were also less likely to deteriorate.

Not only does life happen at a higher speed today, but we replace things at breakneck pace too. A few decades ago, we would have grouped items into perishables and long-term purchases. Perishables might last from a few days (food, cosmetics) to a maximum of one or two years (clothes, underwear). Long-term purchases were meant to last from 10 to 20 years, or a lifetime (car, house, watch, furniture, etc.).

The greatest marketing trick we face today is that companies slowly transform long-term purchases into perishables, and they make us believe that it's for our own good. Change your car every two years. Change your apartment and move to a better neighborhood. Buy more watches to match your outfit, refurnish your rooms often. There is nothing bad about these changes if someone can afford them without getting into a lifetime of debt, but most people can't. This causes them misery, stress, anxiety mixed with feelings of inferiority, and unhappiness.

The other byproduct of overconsumption is the belief system behind it. In bank commercials, they literally show people being happy when they get their new house, and those who don't get that new house are sad and depressed. In shampoo commercials, those who have nice, clean hair are loved by others, while those who don't are ignored. People wearing the newest fashion trend are cool and admired. Those who don't are not.

Who doesn't want to be happy, loved, and cool? We all do, of course, so we just buy and buy and buy. And we choke on the dust.

Some stuff we never end up wearing or using. The best example is that wretched massage chair my parents bought as an "exceptional deal." They never used it, and since it occupied a lot of space, they took it to the cellar. One day, some burglars broke in the cellar stealing a lot of things — the massage chair included. This was 10 years ago, but my parents still sob about that chair — its cost and the "what ifs" they imagined around the useless chair. "What if we bought a bigger house? It would have been a great tool then."

"What if I get back pain? It would be great then." I sincerely feared they would buy a new one to compensate their fictional losses.

But mass consumption — and the fear of losing possessions — spills over and creates massive damage in many areas apart from our own soul. Cheap labor exploitation in developing countries grows and grows, since multinational companies can't make cuts for profit anywhere else than on the lowest level of production: the workers. Did you know that when you see "Made in Bangladesh" on your shirt, the company paid approximately 30 cents for its production in the factory? And that the hourly wage of a garment worker in Bangladesh is about 24 cents?

The environment also suffers under the massive pollution caused by production and waste elimination. There is a Netflix documentary on the topic of mass production and consumption and their "side effects" called *The True Cost*. It is an eye-opening documentary. Its purpose isn't necessarily to change one's habits completely, but it implores us to at least have some perspective and awareness of the deep scars our consumerist world can create.

THE PURPOSE OF THIS BOOK

You bought *Minimalist Makeover*, therefore I assume you have had enough with clutter invading your life. You want to become a more mindful consumer and have a more organized life.

The idea of minimalism became very popular recently — probably as a peaceful revolution against mass consumption. In my previous book, *Less Mess Less Stress*, I presented what minimalism means according to my understanding. I gave tactics and strategies based on my personal experience on how to declutter your mind, relationship, and surroundings in order to achieve your tailor-made minimalist life.

This book presents you four alternative ways to introduce minimalism into your life and reduce mental or physical clutter around you. Some of these methods are older than you and me, and as a matter of fact, older than American culture itself, dating back to Viking times.

I believe that in order to change and improve something, it is vital to know the history of that particular thing. Knowing the history helps us to detect weaknesses and see where improvements can be made. I'll be talking a little about the history and heritage of the methods I will present you.

After a historical walkthrough, I will present the method itself, and provide you with practical examples of how can you improve and downsize your clutter. At the end of each method, I will also talk about the criticism of the method. Knowing opposing opinions can strengthen your argument or help you see things from a different angle. All in all, I will give you four complex minimalist approaches with historical background, practical application, and possible downsides to contemplate. Act upon the parts that are helpful to you and create your own definition of minimalist, simple living.

The four methods are the following:
- The Japanese KonMari method
- The Japanese Wabi-sabi method
- The Swedish Lagom lifestyle
- The Danish Hygge lifestyle

These four methods won't exhaust the meaning of minimalism by far. However, they provide a more global perspective on what minimalism means. These days, the market is filled with books that tell you only the basics of decluttering: throw out what you don't need, donate, downsize, buy the milk in bulk to save at the groceries, and so on. However, they fail to explain the philosophy behind these actions.

Having an organized and balanced life is a form of art and self-expression. It's something you do because you believe in it, because you feel it gives you something valuable, not because today's hipster Zeitgeist tells you so. The values I'm about to present are much older than the New Age minimalism-craze. Learn about them, invite them in — and if they resonate with your inner artist, embrace them.

CHAPTER 1: THE JAPANESE WAY OF DECLUTTERING

History and Heritage

What is the first nation that comes to your mind when I say organized, clean, and tidy? Most people's gut answer is probably Japan, and I bet it's not only because of Marie Kondo's bestselling book, *The Life-Changing Magic of Tidying Up*. The book is the consequence, rather than the cause, of Japan's well-founded reputation.

Building this reputation started long before us, the mighty Europeans, even considered taking a bath — occasionally. It was a common belief that water washes away luck. You could smell someone before you saw them during Europe's Middle Ages. So ladies, does getting saved by a knight still sound appealing?

Chinese historians characterized Japanese as clean in the third century. In the 16th century, when the Portuguese first arrived on the shores of Japan and began trade negotiations in Nagasaki, they also left some memoirs endorsing the Japanese as very tidy.

Japanese cleanliness is not surprising for many reasons. First and foremost, it is an island chain, and therefore the prevention of spreading illnesses was crucial for them. Hygiene kept them healthy and less exposed to epidemics that, as a worst-case scenario, could eradicate an entire island population. Also, their climate has high humidity in summer, and they are susceptible to many natural calamities that also made them hygiene-cautious.

They are blessed with an abundance of natural hot springs ("onsen," in Japanese). Based on the data of the Onsen Association and Statista, there are more than 27,000 onsens in Japan.[iv]

Apart from sensible safety precautions, religion also played a big part in Japanese cleanliness habits. Bathing was, and still is, an important part in both Buddhism and Shintoism — the two main Japanese religious beliefs. They associate good powers with cleanliness and evil with dirtiness. There are purification rituals in Shinto shrines to this day. People wash their hands before prayer because God (Kami) is in everybody and everything, and therefore they must be clean for prayers. Before the 17th century when public baths started to spread, Buddhist temples provided bathing possibilities to the less wealthy.

During the Edo period in the 17th century, public baths ("sento") started to spread. In 1591, the first two opened in Osaka and Edo (present-day Tokyo). By the Meiji Restoration in 1868, there were at least 600 sentos in Tokyo alone. By 1960, there were over 23,000 sentos all over Japan. These places were like the Roman baths of old; they were the main places where people gathered to chatter, discuss ideas, and make deals.[v]

Today, people have their own baths in their homes. However, **around 1,650 sentos are still functioning in Tokyo.** Some of them have adapted to tourist demands and offer exotic services such as jungle scenes, cherry blossom decorations, and other types of enjoyment. Now that almost every family has a bath, the Japanese are even more obsessed with cleanliness. Compared to their bathing demands, foreigners (gaijin) are no match. Therefore, Japanese often consider gaijin rather dirty and undemanding.

When I was planning to visit Japan, I was browsing through Booking.com for low-cost accommodations. I was surprised to see that most of them still don't have bathtub or shower inside. Where the habitant can find the closest sento is listed in the description, as well as how much it costs — and, believe it or not, whether they accept people with tattoos. So as much as it pained me, I had to opt for a not-so-low-cost place when I visited because of my tattoos. Before you judge the Japanese for being judgmental (see the paradox here?), disliking tattoos is a cultural thing.

Did you know?

During the long history of Japan, tattoos were connected to many unpleasant things. There were tattoos serving punitive purposes, meted out to label and punish people for indiscretions. Some tattoos were meant to distinguish social classes. Tattoos were also used by the working class as a way of self-expression and self-protection. Some tattoos had special, protective power —they thought.

And of course, there is the story of the infamous yakuza gangsters getting them.

In the modern era, tattoos have been labeled as a sign of being a gangster, which is why Japanese people are wary of them. However, most people who get tattoos aren't criminals. Many tattoos even feature typical Asian art elements like dragons or koi fish.

Home Organizing Style

The cleanliness of Japanese homes and environments was taken just as seriously over the decades as their bodies. In restaurants, teahouses, and even karaoke bars, the waiters offer a hot, wet towel ("oshibori") for the guests on their arrival, after each meal, and even after they've returned from the restrooms.

From movies like *The Last Samurai* or *Memoirs of a Geisha*, even those who are not particularly interested in Japanese culture know that before entering a Japanese house, one should always remove their shoes. Remember Tom Cruise marching inside with his dirty boots in the movie *The Last Samurai*? People looked cross with him for a reason. Cleanliness goes as far as cleaning the dog's or cat's legs before letting them enter the house (Japanese pet owners also bathe their pets every day, or at least groom them with some mega-hygienic solution, according to Ikko, my Japanese friend).

The structure of a Japanese home is very simple. There isn't much furniture, but there are many storage items for organizing everything flawlessly. For a Japanese person, having a messy home is a great shame. I feel a little off if one of my friends comes over when my flat is not spotless, but shame in the Japanese sense is much more than that.

Japanese homes are rather small. Since the island has its natural limits, but is highly populated, the average Japanese person doesn't have as spacious a home as an American. Spaces are tiny, so having a good storage system to keep order is essential. In Japan, there are not many sidewalks in residential areas; therefore, they separate public and private space with a traditional (or regular) roof gate.

The houses usually have a step-up entryway to keep the home dry in the rainy season. Humidity reaches its peak from June to July. As a result, Japanese architecture is designed to protect people, including raised floors and dwellings to make the house more airy and open.

There is a transitional area between the outdoors and the house where people exchange their shoes for slippers. When stepping on the tatami floor, they remove the slippers as well.

The interior design of a traditional Japanese home is dominated by wood. The wooden surfaces are never painted. Natural-colored wooden furniture and decorations give a minimalist angle to the rooms. Tatami flooring is more popular among wealthy families, since the woven igusa (a type of grass tatami is made of) is quite pricey. Tatami flooring is cool in summer and warm in winter.

Japanese traditional beds, futons, are usually stored in a closet during the day, allowing some of their rooms to serve multiple purposes. They can use the room as both a living room and bedroom, depending on the part of the day. Remember, they have small houses.

When it comes to wall décor, paintings and artwork were originally painted in monochrome. A few simple strokes of the brush in outline could symbolize mountains and forests. In opposition to Western art, which is known to use vivid colors in an explicit way, Japanese art is more subtle. Japanese people appreciate "the spirit of the art." Their sense of beauty and aesthetic value comes from feelings, rather than logic. In other words, they consider something beautiful because they feel it is beautiful, not because it is logical to consider it beautiful. Their aesthetic sense is very subjective.[vi]

Did you know?

To better understand a country's mentality, it is good to take a look at their everyday people's habits, tales, and daily life. I read a few Japanese folktales, and the commonality in them was the portrayal of two kinds of beauty: the visual and the emotional. Their folktales often emphasized the beauty of the seasons in parallel to the hero's or heroine's emotional world.

One of the most well-known Japanese folktales is called *A Bush Warbler and the House.* The story is about a wood chucker who finds a nice house among plum blossom trees. Entering the house, he sees a beautiful woman. She must leave, so she lets the wood chucker stay in her house under the condition that he may not look into the other reception rooms. He can't keep his promise and takes a look into the rooms. Each room has a set of nice furniture and paintings of the four seasons. In the last room, he finds three eggs.

He picks them up, then accidentally drops them.

At this moment, the woman comes home and faces the damage done. She starts crying and transforms into a bush warbler. She bitterly sings that she misses her children. When she flies away, the nice house disappears and the wood chucker finds himself on the field again.

On one hand, we can't miss the beautiful portrait of the plum blossoms and the picturesque beauty of the four seasons. The appearance of the bush warbler gives the peak of the visuals of this folktale. We can also feel the emotional beauty of this tale: the woman is patient, compassionate, and forgiving. She does not seek revenge for the murder of her children. It's likely that the feeling of shame she experienced at having her true nature exposed was greater than her rage. The story is an indication of how feelings of shame and patience were expected and admired among women in old Japan.

The shame of exposing someone's true nature, for example, like seeing his or her house when it's not clean enough, or having exhibitionist or out-of-ordinary elements, is still strong in Japan. This is one reason why the Japanese are not famous for pompous decorations and designs, but more withdrawn and simple ones.

Even in today's modern storytelling, like anime (animated movies), we can often encounter this artistic duality: the expression of beauty and emotions. Japanese people are, by culture, less expressive in everyday life, and thus they pour their feelings in highly emotional stories. I must confess, many anime shows leave my eyes wet.

There is another important determining factor of the Japanese way of organizing, or Japanese minimalism. This factor is not a visible aspect, but an internal one — modesty and humility. These are the most important aspects of good behavior in Japan. It illustrates in their way of living as well. Not only do people live in serene circumstances, but those who are wealthy are also expected to be modest. There is a famous Japanese proverb that reflects this expectation: "The nail that sticks up gets hammered down." In other words, if someone shows off their abilities to excess, they will be pushed down by others. This proverb reflects the Japanese group ideology, but younger generations tend to be less and less respectful toward old traditions.

With the Meiji Restoration and after World War II, Japan opened up culturally, compared to their previous attitude, and tried to keep up with Western habits. They started wearing blue jeans (their traditional kimonos are now worn on special occasions and during ceremonies), listen to rock music, eat fast food, and sleep in a bed. They even eat with a knife and fork. Western lifestyle started to be accepted, particularly during the Allied Occupation. Even if their habits and cleaning rituals may still seem a bit rigid to us, compared to Edo times, Japan became keener to adopt Western habits.

We might ask ourselves where we can find original Japanese culture with its deep sense of beauty.

As with every nation, Japan is changing, and their habits, art, and house decoration style is keeping up with the latest trends to explore the most efficient possibilities.

I think it is important to understand one nation's history before judging their way of living, even if you want to adopt only a small part of their daily habits. Knowing the background of anything you want to master helps you achieve a better understanding. You'll see a habit more sensibly if you can understand why it was necessary to adopt it. Knowing the history of something also gives you perspective. Knowing how the habit started, why it started, and thinking about it more in-depth will help you come up with

new solutions that can improve that habit —
or transform the habit to fit your life.

Lastly, knowing the history can make you less judgmental. If you're willing to see a different nation's habits objectively, without mixing them with your nation's ideologies, you'll realize they can make sense. Try to put yourself in that nation's shoes and accept that what they believe is the norm they grew up with. Doing this, you'll realize that you could also relate to their behavior if you grew up with them.

Leave the nationality bias on the porch for a moment. Imagine yourself being Japanese, regardless of where you come from. Read more information about them, watch some movies, or listen to some traditional Japanese songs. If you'd like to simplify your life in the Japanese way, it will be much more exciting and easy if you become a little bit Japanese yourself.

Why? You won't have the feeling of "us and them," just a free flow of acceptance. Select the habits that fit your world and desired lifestyle and leave out all the rest, but try to be as open-minded as possible. You don't have to transform into a Japanese person to live a Japanese-like life. However, approaching the Japanese lifestyle with judgment and prejudice will cloud your objectivity, and may prevent you from taking the best parts and improving them to your taste.

I must note that being judgmental and prejudiced is not a helpful quality to have regarding anything, if your aim is to improve and have a wider perspective.

What do I mean when I say "select the habits"? If you live in California, for example, there is a high chance you won't need step-up doorways, or elevated floors and dwellings, since there's generally not much rain. However, you can keep the Japanese interior design feature of tatami flooring, if you like it.

You can behave serenely, if you feel that's closer to your heart. Take what you like from the cultural and organizational aspects and improve them to fit your lifestyle. It's your life, and you should make it as happy for yourself as humanly possible.

Accepting other's traditions is not always easy. Let me share with you a few personal experiences from my visit to Japan.

I was visiting my best friend, who currently lives in Osaka. We went out for breakfast. I usually eat something light, like yoghurt. Since I was a child, when I opened the yoghurt, I licked the stuff off the lid. I grew up pretty poor, and leaving so much invaluable substance on the lid to me seemed like a huge waste. I finished the lid, and with self-contentment, I started eating my yoghurt. I observed that people sitting nearby looked at me with a kind of disgust in their eyes. I didn't get it until my friend enlightened me that in Japan, it was impolite and unhygienic to do what I just did. I felt a little embarrassed.

Even if at home nobody would care, objectively looking at my situation, I was a grown-ass woman licking a yoghurt lid like a child in a patriarchal country with serious cleanliness fetishism. I was inconsiderate. However, I couldn't help thinking of what would they say about my plate after I'd eaten a dripping Nutella pancake.

Another near-situation I caused in a restaurant was when my friend and some Japanese colleagues went out for dinner with me. We ate some dinner boxes with salad, tempura, rice, and miso soup. At the end, to help the waiter, I wanted to put my plates onto each other when one of my friend's colleagues, Omi San, stopped me, slowly shaking his head. As it turned out, it was an insult to stack the dirty plates upon one other. On one hand, I offended the waiter by taking his job, on the other hand again, the cleanliness. The plates get washed anyway, so I was confused for a moment, but then I tried this at home, and I was much happier not having to scrub the oil from both sides of the plate instead of one.

In Japan, especially in the humid season, people carry a little handkerchief with them to dry their sweat. They have a handkerchief for their head and neck, and a different handkerchief for their armpits and other parts. First, I was very surprised when I saw them discreetly drying their armpits, but then I decided to try it. Nowhere in the world would this be less awkward than in Japan, I thought. And guess what? I loved it. I felt much better during the day not having to fight against my sweat, taking *Titanic*-inspired Kate-and-Leo prow poses in random places to dry my armpits. I bought like, 10 Japanese handkerchiefs and gave them to my friends, spreading the word of my newfound habit. Now we are the weird white people on the street with sakura-patterned handkerchiefs drying our armpits like champions, wearing colorful silk blouses without being stressed about the sweat stains we might get.

I could write a book full of stories about the weird practical habits I learned in Japan, but I know you're impatient to read about the de facto decluttering and organizing habits. In the following pages, I will present to you the highlights of the KonMari Method and the Wabi-sabi Method. I will be as detailed as necessary to give you an applicable tool to improve your order-keeping skills. If you feel you need more information, or just simply want to get more in-depth with any of the two methods, I suggest you read more about them.

The KonMari Method

Marie Kondo exploded in the United States, and I kept wondering why. Why, above all countries in the world, would the most consumerist, stuff-loving one get hooked on the KonMari Method? Let's face it, people, the US is all about big spaces, big cars, big meals, and a lot of stuff. How on Earth could a strict, no-excuses elimination method take off here?

The answer I came up with is that it was precisely because they have lots of stuff that is almost choking them. The US is a welfare country. A considerable amount of the population has not recently experienced deep poverty — on a country level — the way we did in the post-communist bloc. As a result, people in the US don't usually feel that obsessive attachment to their stuff.

To people who had nothing growing up and felt the constant terror of the communist regime, Eastern Europeans find it stupid to give away all of their stuff when they finally get it. I can strongly feel this mentality in my parents, and everybody their age. It was even truer for my grandparents. Hoarding culture is still present in ex-communist and communist countries such as China. For people who lacked in their infancy, accumulating stuff provides a sense of security for them in adulthood.

My grandfather didn't allow me to throw away plastic bottles and yoghurt cups because we never knew when the (by then non-existent) collective would come to power again and socialize our lands. We would need those bottles to secretly grow vegetables in the basement to survive. I bet no one in the US ever had a sleepless night with the same fears as my grandpa did, unless someone like my grandpa moved there. He probably had an iron fence and a separate storage space for his plastic bottle collection because he wasn't playing around with tomato security.

After having this epiphany about the whys of the KonMari method's popularity, I figured that the United States is the best place where one can start such a movement. I don't think I'm exaggerating when I say "movement." Thousands and thousands of people in the United States decided to go hands-on and start "kondoing" their lives. They had the extra stuff, the open-mindedness, and the constant drive for improvement. A little Japanese minimalism here, a little American willingness to improve there, seasoned with good marketing and a well-selected problem, with a huge demand for fixation and boom, and the recipe for a best-selling book was ready. *The Life Changing Magic of Tidying Up* was translated into many languages, including English and Chinese, and is sold in more than 30 countries.

Who is Marie Kondo?

She is a Japanese organizing consultant and best-selling author. She was selected as one of the 100 most influential people in 2015 by *TIME* magazine.

After reading about her early life, I think she is one of those inborn geniuses who possess talent in a particular area. This area is her organizing skill. She obsessed over organizing from a very early age. In elementary school when her classmates played outside, she was organizing the bookshelves of the classroom. She took care of keeping her family's home organized too.

One day, she had a realization: she was too focused on what could she throw out. She realized that simply throwing things out wouldn't make her or other people genuinely happy. Simply throwing stuff away didn't give people a philosophy, or a heartfelt, genuine feeling that they were doing the right thing. So she shifted perspective. From that moment on, she focused on what she wanted to keep. The items that could provoke a "spark of joy" in her should be kept, and the rest should be discarded.

This shifted view on organizing takes us to the essence of the KonMari Method's philosophy. First, we have to gather our belongings. Choosing one category at a time, we have to select and keep only those things that "spark joy" (make us happy via our strong emotional bond to it). After this, we have to choose a place for them and commit to keeping them in that place.

The KonMari Method's basics perfectly reflect the old Japanese mentality I was telling you about in the historical preamble. Their sense of beauty and importance in art (and the art of organizing) is subjective. It is not always logical, but emotionally based. The "spark of joy," in my opinion, is the modern translation of this old beauty concept.

The goal of the KonMari Method isn't to reduce the items of in your house to under 100, or to throw away or donate as many things as possible. The goal is to create a practical environment where you surround yourself with the things you love.

There are some rules in Kondo's book. Some steps have to be executed in a certain order for optimal results. According to Kondo, we have two tasks when decluttering: discarding items and finding a place for the rest, in this order.

One should finish discarding the unneeded and unloved items first, and only then move on to the organizing part. Why? If the discarding is not quick and radical enough, we won't feel the sweeping notion of change, and we might get tired of fighting clutter without clear improvement and give up halfway through. In Kondo's experience, a "quick discarding period" is around six months. Depending on how many things you own and how quickly you can say goodbye to things, this time can be significantly reduced. However, do not start thinking about where you will put the items you keep until you're finished with discarding the unnecessary ones.

Another important step before you start getting rid of your things is to have a clear vision of what you want to achieve with decluttering. Saying "I want less mess" is not strong enough. "I want to live in a house with clear floors and just a few decorations, such as some candles, my favorite books, and some plants. My bedroom should look like a hotel room. I want my bed to be the most comfortable part of the house with memory pillows and fluffy blankets, and I want to match the bed sheets with the curtains. I want candles and incense in my bathroom. I want to store all my items in drawers and wardrobes that are not transparent. The less I see, the better. I want to have a clean walkway throughout my entire house." This is a clear goal and a detailed vision. Having this, you'll know what you need to give away and what you can keep to actually get there. The more you think about your goal, you'll realize "the whole point in discarding and keeping things is to be happy."[vii]

Kondo recommends tidying by category and not by location. For example, you might start with clothing and appliances, instead of the bedroom and kitchen. This way, you can avoid keeping two of the same thing. Let's say you have scissors in the kitchen drawer, and a pair in the study drawer too. If you go room by room, you may overlook the fact that you have two identical scissors, and you won't do as deep a tidying as you're looking for.

How do you discard things with the help of "joy sparks"? Choose a category of items and gather them into one place. Pick up each individual item and ask yourself, "Does this spark joy?" "Does this make me happy?" It may sound odd first, and it isn't a quick process, but you don't have to finish it in one day. With practice, it becomes a habit. Surrounding yourself with things you love and learning how to keep them in order is an invaluable practice for a stress-free life. The point is to focus on what you have and love; items that make you happy, satisfied, and grateful. If in tidying you focus on the negative, the struggle, and the loss, you will poison your mood.

Get rid of dysfunctional items (broken, outdated, useless things) first. This should be easy. It is more difficult to discard things that have functional, informational, or emotional value, especially if they are hard to replace. Kondo advises to start tidying with the clothing category. It is the best choice, since clothes can be replaced easily. Also, making the first steps quickly and effortlessly will warm you up so when you get to the more difficult decisions, you'll be in a flow state.

Somewhere in your discarding process, you'll inevitably bump into things that won't make you feel a spark of joy. Rationally, you know they are useless (or at least, you don't use them), but you still can't get rid of them. This can be emotional attachment or rationalization, like you might need it later, it was expensive, or it will be a good fit for your cousin when she grows up. Your brain can be very cunning when it comes to rationalizing why should you keep something. When you come across such an item, Marie Kondo's advice is to think about the feelings you had when you purchased it.

Were you happy when you bought it? Did you think that it was cool, but you never used it? What's the situation with it today? Your style may have changed, so you don't need that pink shirt. Or perhaps you became a vegetarian, so you no longer need the cookbook about the *1001 Best Meat Dishes*. Realize that this object already completed its role in your life — at the very least, it showed you something you're not. It guided you so you could realize which style doesn't fit you anymore or what dish you shouldn't cook. Thank this item for what it did for you and let it go. Maybe Jim, the butcher at the corner shop, would kill for that cookbook.

Kondo's practice can prove to be very effective for organizing closets. We ladies can develop irrational attachments to clothing: "My husband bought it." "It was very expensive." "It will be good when I lose some pounds," etc. We keep on filling space with more and more clothes we don't wear. In my previous book, *Less Mess Less Stress,* I presented my best method of how to get rid of things.

Now, I'll present Marie Kondo's best tips on how to store the "surviving clothing items." After getting rid of the items that don't spark joy, it is critical to find a place for every piece of clothing to avoid re-cluttering. In many cases, people discard a cartload of items just to make space for new clutter. Clever, stackable storage solutions do more harm than good when it comes to hoarding prevention. The goal here isn't to store thousands of pieces of clutter smartly, but to have the necessary amount of loved items that are just as easy to put away as they are to locate.

Kondo encourages developing good folding techniques instead of buying smart storages. Rather than randomly throwing things in a drawer, clothes should stand upright — for multiple reasons. On one hand, the more folds they have, the less wrinkled they will become. On the other hand, folding is space-saving. Lastly, it will grant your clothes the respect they deserve for their service. By taking on the burden to nicely fold each item, you'll show appreciation and proper treatment.

How to Store Your Underwear

To me, it seemed an unnecessary waste of time to fold underwear, but once I tried, I realized how much nicer and cleaner my drawer looked, so I made it a habit to fold my underwear.

First, lay your underwear flat in front of you. Then fold in half lengthwise, and crotch to waistband. Fold in the sides. Fold over the crotch again so it stands upright.

How to Store Your Socks

I know you love to make a ball of your socks and throw it at your spouse or sibling like a snowball, but I have bad news for you: they'll look like spring rolls. Lay socks flat as a pair, one sock on top of the other. Fold the toe inward, an inch from the top. Then fold them in to the center. Finally, fold them in half so they stand upright.

How to Store Your Trousers

I'm a trouser addict. Some people hoard shoes, some bags — I hoard trousers. I succeeded in getting rid of some, but they spark a fountain of joy of me. What can I do?

And more importantly, how can I store them effectively? Marie told me.

Lay the trousers flat. Fold the left leg over the right. Fold in the crotch. Fold over the bottom toward the waist, leaving an inch of space. Fold inward until the trouser stands upright.

How to Store Your Shirts

This will be a long one. You can always search for videos on YouTube for the visual demonstration of the folding method, if you can't do it with my description.

Lay the shirt down flat in front of you. Fold in the right side with the sleeve flat. Fold back the sleeve halfway. Do the same on the left side. Then repeat the sleeve fold so you're left with a rectangle. Fold in the neckline an inch away from the hem. Fold halfway. Fold in half again until it stands upright.

How to Store Long-sleeved Shirts and Sweaters

It's less complicated than it sounds. Lay the sweater flat with the sleeves spread out. Fold in the right side with the sleeve straight out so it crosses the body. Fold the sleeve over and down so it creates a triangle. Repeat on the left side so you are left with a rectangle. Start from the top and fold inward until it stands upright.

The rolling techniques of Marie Kondo are simple, but magical. Just imagine how you want to prevent papers from creasing. You roll them into a cylinder instead of folding them in halves or quarters.

This picture is of my own wardrobe. The left side is of my socks and bras. In the upper right photo, you can see my long-sleeved shirts on the bottom, my pants in the middle, t-shirts above them, and my sports clothes on the very top. In the bottom right, you can see underwear and more socks.

What can give an exquisite look to your drawer is to position your nicely folded clothes in order of color. To me, this would mean from white to black (White-Yellow-Orange-Red-Purple-Blue-Turquoise-Green-Gray-Black). You can choose a different ordering structure. This rainbow-like array can be heartwarming when you look at your drawer.

If you've read *The Life Changing Magic of Tidying Up* by Marie Kondo, you probably noticed that she treats objects with great respect. The methods she developed for discarding and storing both involve showing gratitude and respect to the object that faithfully served us and will still serve us in the future. This kind of humble, respectful attitude mirrors the type of Japanese attitude I briefly described in the History and Heritage section.

Western culture doesn't afford objects such appreciation. It might be difficult for us to understand why we should treat objects with respect, since they can't feel anything. I believe that showing respect, appreciation, and gratitude genuinely makes us happy. The more we practice gratitude, the happier and more fulfilled we'll be. My dad once told me that if you have gratitude in your heart, you can't feel any sense of lacking. If you give thanks for what you have, and acknowledge you are blessed to have things you can give away, any sense of scarcity will leave your system.

To me, this is the greatest takeaway of Marie Kondo's book: Be grateful for what you have and treat it well. Treating your surroundings with grace and goodness adds up to treating yourself the same way.

Criticism of the KonMari Method

When we would like to introduce a new habit into our lives, it is wise to examine the counterarguments regarding it. The whole picture is never black or white, and knowing opposing opinions helps us create a more realistic expectation of the subject of our examination.

The KonMari method is compact, well-thought-out, and easily applicable, if there is a strong determination behind it. However, it might not be a good choice for everybody.

I come from a family who lost everything during both World War II and communism. I can say from experience that for my parents and grandparents, parting from things is not as easy as it is for me, the child who didn't experience such severe losses.

My great-grandparents were German (not "evil" ones, but peaceful farmers and clothing shop owners in a small village). When the Soviet Union invaded Eastern Europe and Germany, everybody who was German had a very good reason to fear for their lives. My great-grandmother and my grandmother hid in a basement while the Russians stormed over the countryside, taking all the goods, raping women, and burning the fields after them. I'm not even saying that Soviets are the evil ones —this is how wars work, unfortunately.

I learned from my grandmother, who was only seven years old back then, that the Russian troops stole everything from their shop, burned their fields, and a bomb ruined half of their home — and the soldiers took her father (my great-grandfather) as a hostage to the Soviet Union. My grandmother was left with nothing. My great-grandmother had pneumonia and died a few years later. Luckily, the village had a good community spirit and helped each other out. Still, I feel that my grandmother came from a time and place I can't even comprehend.

The post-war and cold war years left severe marks in my grandmother. She had a great attachment to those few things they had been left with — especially memories of her parents. My great-grandfather was one of the few German hostages who could make it home — alive. After seven years of horror, working in a Soviet gulag (a system of labor camps maintained in the Soviet Union), he returned home to find his wife dead and his child living on the good will of the village people. He was a very strong-willed man and didn't let himself crumble.

The barber of the village had died recently, so he jumped in to become the new barber. He worked until he died at the age of 86. If he'd lived two years longer, I could have met him.

My grandmother's problems didn't end with her father's return. The family went through another shock when the communist party socialized their lands, which had been their main source of income. She had such a deep fear of scarcity that she grew to appreciate every single item they had, even when communism collapsed and scarcity was not an issue anymore. She installed this mentality in my mother too.

My grandfather had a similar (although not so tragic) background, so together with my grandmother, they responded to the trauma they'd experienced by holding onto things. Both became hoarders. They went out every Thursday to the village flea market, looking for random trinkets to buy "for the difficult times to come." They kept everything, from trash (they burned some in winter) to receipts and yoghurt cans.

My mother is slightly more practical, but not much different. Even today, when she gets her pension, the first thing she does is go to the shop to refill our food stock. Canned food, 10 loaves of bread in the freezer, gallons and gallons of water stored in the basement — she's prepared for the apocalypse. I keep telling her that nothing bad will happen in the next 30 days, but she is relentless — this is *the way* she feels safe.

My family isn't the only one that possesses this kind of mentality. Most of the immigrant families in the US experienced similar losses. We have a refugee crisis today — especially in Europe, where people have a rucksack full of things left from a two-story house.

People who have lost everything don't find anything glamorous in giving their precious belongings away. It has a different value for them — each individual item is a symbol of freedom and proof that hard times are behind them. For people who have a history of needing to decide whether an item is necessary for survival, instead of whether or not it sparks joy, the concept of downsizing their home might seem ridiculous or insulting.

Last year, I threw out my dad's newspaper collection when he wasn't home. He had been hoarding newspapers for almost 10 years, and they'd piled up in three thick lines from floor to ceiling in our storage room. They'd started to smell and certainly were dusty. I was so happy to finally get rid of them. When my dad came home and saw the crime I'd committed, he started crying. I felt so ashamed. I learned an important lesson that day: you can't force de-cluttering, minimalism, or the KonMari method on everybody. Some people simply can't accept it.

Of course, for people who are confident that they can easily replace the things they part with, it's easy to embrace decluttering and minimalism. It is an act of trust, at the end of the day. Trust that everything can get back to normal, if the decluttering project doesn't deliver the desired outcome. It is easy to see items as clutter when we are sure that throwing them out does not have definitive consequences. For someone who knows what it feels like to lose everything, the idea of cheerfully checking whether or not personal belongings inspire happiness is borderline disrespectful, and at the very least stupid.

Taking into consideration the story I've just told, I concluded that the criticism of the KonMari method could be the seemingly ignorant approach to some important aspects of human nature, like the irrational emotional imprinting of loss many people have.

Surely, those who don't like it shouldn't do it. Those who like it should be considerate about those who don't see the KonMari method as life-changing magic. As Marie Kondo herself said, one should clean his or her personal space with the intent of giving a good example that others can decide whether to follow.

The Wabi-sabi Method

Simplicity and elegance are the main characteristics of Japanese aesthetic values. These have been the dominant features of people's lives since ancient times. Traditional Japanese architecture possesses an elegant look with its empty spaces, matte and natural colors, and lack of ornamentation. These qualities apply to Japanese arts and literature as well. Wabi-sabi is the Japanese phrase that expresses this kind of aesthetic feature.

However, wabi-sabi can't be summarized as simplicity and elegance. It has much deeper characteristics that are almost impossible to define with Western words. For non-Japanese, wabi-sabi is easier to understand if we let the concept into our lives with our senses, not our minds.

Why Do I Think This?

I recently traveled to Lisbon were I visited the local oceanarium. They have two exhibitions, a permanent one and a temporary one. After a long and exhausting tour among the permanent exhibition's wonders, I was quite reluctant to visit the temporary one. However, I felt that I should go and see it since I was there. I didn't even know what the exhibition was about, but it was included in my ticket, so I entered.

The exhibition was about the heritage of a Japanese landscape photographer, Takashi Amano. He traveled all over the world's forests and captured photos of the most imposing landscapes. Inspired by the colorful, simple, imperfect beauty of nature, Takashi Amano started designing and creating freshwater aquariums and became the international master thereof. His artwork is known as "nature aquariums." What makes his work truly special is the combination of Japanese gardening techniques with the wabi-sabi concept. His works aim to recreate nature in its simple, imperfect beauty. Takashi Amano strongly believed that observing nature closely and seeing its imperfect perfection could help us to better understand the world. If we gain a better understanding, we can learn how to preserve it.

The exhibition itself was very relaxing and beautiful. Just sitting and watching the well-composed aquariums, I entered into a meditative state. It was so calming to sit there and watch the fish peacefully swim in their artificial habitat. They are not complaining about it, they don't feel the need to declutter, and they don't feel dissatisfied with what they have or what they lack. They accept and explore all they've got: the aquarium.

We humans are so much luckier. We have so many choices. We have it all, but we hardly ever stop thinking about what we lack. Most of our time is spent on things we don't have yet. We run ahead of the moment, trying to grasp our future wishes while we let precious moments pass us by. If we'd spend half as much time giving thanks for what we do have as we spend on praying for the things we don't, our lives would be much happier.

We constantly search for the imperfections in our lives instead of focusing on the perfections in our beautiful, imperfect lives. The wabi-sabi method, in my opinion, teaches us to accept and love life in its imperfect wholeness.

The wabi-sabi method is the permanent mind-decluttering solution. It is more than a method; it is a lifestyle philosophy.

What is Wabi-sabi, Exactly?

Literally translated, "wabi" means simplicity. It is both an aesthetic and moral value. The concept's roots date back to the medieval eremitic traditions. These emphasize "a simple, austere type of beauty, and a serene, transcendental frame of mind, yet also points to the enjoyment of a quiet, leisurely life, free from worldly concerns." (Ohbunsha Kogojiten, 1988.)[viii]

"Sabi" is the beauty of age and wear. This term was also coined in medieval times. Sabi started to develop aesthetic qualities thanks to the spread of Buddhism. People started to change their attitude toward the deplorable condition of aging and look at it as something natural and embraceable.

In ancient times, people used the words *wabi* and *sabi* to express the difficulty and dissatisfaction with their lives. With the spread of Zen Buddhism, people slowly changed their minds regarding these concepts and started to contemplate what was beyond simple, plain existence.

In short, wabi-sabi is an aesthetic philosophy rooted in Zen Buddhism. The concept of *mu* ("emptiness") is central to Zen. It was a key factor in the evolution of wabi-sabi. "Zen does not regard 'nothingness' as a state of the absence of objects but rather affirms the existence of the unseen behind the empty space: 'Everything exists in emptiness: flowers, the moon in the sky, beautiful scenery.'"[ix](Ikeno, Osamu, Davies, Roger. *The Japanese Mind.*)

Wabi-sabi was particularly evident in the tea ceremonies during the Kamakura period. They were rituals of purity and simplicity. Tea was served in handmade bowls, and masters prized bowls that had irregular shapes, or uneven glaze, cracks, and represented beauty in its intentional imperfection. The bowls were valued because of — not in spite of — their flaws and cracks.

Imagine what a life you could have if you learned to appreciate the flaws and cracks. It would be beautiful. The Japanese philosophy of beauty is subjective and based on feelings. It accepts flaws and natural imperfections, and that's what makes something whole and real.

I found it very interesting that wabi-sabi played an important role in the poetry of the Edo period. The world-famous Japanese "haiku" poems were greatly influenced by the spirit of wabi-sabi. Matsuo Basho, maybe the greatest poet of the Edo period, used the word "sabi" for the first time in the context we discuss it: "It is marvelous. The color of sabi emerges well."[x]

In Western culture, "simplicity" means two things: a pejorative label for simple-mindedness, or a life flawlessly organized to fake or showcase perfection. In our culture, bringing out the best from our potential, improving a skill to mastery, or striving to be the brightest has value. For us, it is unnatural to seek satisfaction in a concept that values the rust.

We are addicted to perfection. The keywords we look for when buying a product are "perfect," "immediate," "instant," "best," "top," "best-seller," etc. We would probably never buy something that is "imperfect," "eventual," or "the fourth." We know that what is said to be a best-seller might not uniformly help all seven billion people on Earth. We know that any kind of "instant" help, improvement, or solution is rarely so. We know that "perfection" is subjective, and thus it's bold to label anything with this word.

We jump quickly to judgment when we observe imperfections. We focus on them, instead of the value that is much greater than the flaws. As a writer, I often get feedback like, "I didn't read the book because it had typos," or "I can't take the book seriously because of the typos." My judges are correct, there are typos in my books — as a matter of fact, there are very few books by other authors where I didn't detect typos. We writers are humans, after all. Our editors are also humans. I'm not angry with readers who decide not to value my books because of the typos — it's their decision. But what will they be left with? The bitter disappointment caused by a small mistake. They chose to focus on the mistake instead of accepting it and searching for valuable thoughts that could be helpful to them for a lifetime. I'm not saying this out of bitterness — there will always be people who love my work, and there will always be those who don't.

When it comes to home, mind, or emotional decluttering, the same attitude can be detected: people focus on what's bad. The clutter is what's annoying, the things their mind can't complete, like the problems they have in their relationships. In embracing the wabi-sabi mentality, focus on the negative can be shifted.

How You Can Apply the Wabi-sabi Method to Declutter Your Home

A wabi-sabi home has a unique character. It has items that you love and appreciate. If an old piece of furniture has significance to you (sparks joy), but has a scratches and a sticker your child adhered to it, that doesn't mean it's lost its beauty or value. You can shift your focus from the imperfection. Instead of thinking, "This furniture looks like garbage," you can think, "The scratches on this piece are signs of faithful service, and the sticker is a memory of the lovely times of my child's infancy."

Did you know?

The Japanese word for beautiful ("utsukushii") comes from an older meaning that translates to "being loved"?

In wabi-sabi, handmade things have greater value than mainstream market pieces. A clumsy-looking chair made with love has greater value than a shiny plastic one with a posh design. Wabi-sabi embraces natural materials such as stone, wood, metal, and cotton that age with dignity and rustic beauty. Natural colors like green, gray, brown, and other earth tones create an atmosphere of harmony and calmness.

That's not to say wabi-sabi means accepting or embracing clutter. "There is thought and work behind it, not neglect," says Robyn Griggs Lawrence, author of *Simply Imperfect: Revisiting the Wabi-Sabi House*.[xi] Even the most expensive, "perfect" home décor can blend into clutter. You can't realize beauty without mindful discarding of the useless and unused.

Decluttering with wabi-sabi means to create for yourself a simple, rustic, natural environment that gives you tranquility. Mixing wabi-sabi philosophy with the KonMari method's hands-on practicality can create the inspiring, minimalist, and simple environment you're looking for.

How to Apply Wabi-sabi to Declutter Your Mind

According to the wabi-sabi mindset, nothing is perfect, nothing is finished, and nothing lasts. Yet this gives beauty to our imperfect, unfinished, and ever-changing world. What we should strive for is to live our lives authentically. The wabi-sabi mindset challenges us to question and re-evaluate what is truly important in life. If we can leave behind the inauthentic expectations of today's overconsuming society, we can live with less stress and more happiness.

To truly thrive in the wabi-sabi philosophy, you should declutter your environment and mindset. "But I want to use wabi-sabi to declutter, not declutter to be able to use wabi-sabi," you may say. Luckily, you can apply this mindset both ways.

Wabi-sabi teaches us to open our senses and grasp the present moment. Think only when you must, and try to live your life through your senses.

Use your eyes to see the beauty that surrounds you. With your fingers, touch the smooth moss on the stones. Listen to the river rushing restlessly. Taste the deliciousness of a ripe apple. Take a deep breath to catch the sense of your loved one lying next to you. Use your senses to fully engage in life as it happens each moment. This way, you'll find beauty and pleasure in everything that surrounds you.

Try to do this exercise each day. Give yourself five minutes a day to consciously activate your five senses and be in the moment. Do not plan or think too much about it — just give in to your instinctual senses.

Start right now. After you finish reading this paragraph, put the book down. You are in the moment. Close your eyes, inhale, and feel into your body. Leave out every thought and just focus on the action you're performing in this very moment — your breathing. Feel how blessed you are that you're alive and you can breathe; feel into the space around you. You have freedom. You have everything everybody else has on this earth: the richness of this very moment. Feel that you're a part of a whole that is timeless and endless. Even if you are limited in space and time on this earth, you belong to the whole which is endless, and therefore, so are you. Remain in this meditative state for as long as you choose.

Take moments like this as often as you can. Empty your mind of worries and declutter everything that drags you back to past pains, or kicks you to future concerns. I know it is impossible to let go of such thoughts all the time. However, it's not impossible for five to 10 minutes a day. It doesn't matter where you do it — in your own living room, in nature, or while enjoying an activity. What matters is to let go of thoughts and worries, and embrace and find beauty with your five senses wherever you are. The more you practice it, the stronger your wabi-sabi mindset will become. After this practice, you'll feel refreshed and more present. You'll be enabled to authentically enjoy the simple beauty that surrounds you.

How to Apply the Wabi-sabi Method in Relationships

It requires different energy flow and focus when you learn to apply the wabi-sabi method to engage with objects and harmonize your environment, or when you take care of your own mind. When you want to bring this mindset into your relationship where the other party has his or her own thoughts, worries, and emotions, it requires a lot of patience and awareness. The closer you are with your partner, the more open you are with each other, and the easier it is to discover each other's imperfections.

According to Arielle Ford, the wabi-sabi approach to relationships encourages us to "Learn to accept, embrace and even find the gift of your partner's imperfections … finding the perfection in all that is imperfect within them." This is how Ford, author of the book *Wabi Sabi Love: The Ancient Art of Finding Love in Imperfect Relationships,* summarizes the wabi-sabi effect on relationships. In her work, she emphasizes the research-proven truth about the happiest couples being those who focus on what's right and not what's wrong in their relationship. If you give your partner a good reputation to live up to, they will rise to meet it.[xii]

How can you use the best wabi-sabi to connect with your partner? Be compassionate with each other. Don't be harsh and quick to judge. It's just like public speaking: no performer wants to perform poorly on purpose, and no audience wants to listen to an unsuccessful performance. We can also reverse it: all speakers wish to perform well to satisfy the audience, and all audiences wish the speakers to succeed.

Try to approach your relationship with this mindset. Don't assume that your partner performs poorly because he or she wants to. There are smaller or bigger differences between you that create some dissonance, but that only adds a unique angle to your melody. Assume the best. Think that your partner wishes to be the best performer ever, but as with all performers, he or she may be nervous and wasn't born as a professional public speaker. We all need practice.

Show support as the "audience," and give long, heartfelt embraces regularly. Long, close hugs are much better and deeper than the distant pat on the shoulder we sometimes give to our loved ones. Connect on a heart-to-heart level. Even when something goes wrong, don't lose your temper. Instead, focus on how you can move on happily and with love. Each of you are the performers and the audience at the same time. You may have your personal quirks and imperfections. Strive to respond to them with compassion and patience.

Wabi-sabi Today — its Reality and Criticism

The original meaning of wabi-sabi is fading in modern Japan. Some say that it has completely lost its old meaning. People today can't understand the essence as their ancestors did. Tea ceremonies today aren't practiced with such a discipline of mind as they were in medieval times. Rather, the ceremonies serve as a form of entertainment, which has more materialistic motivation behind it. Imitating past customs attracts many curious patrons. The rushing, changed world makes different demands today. People are more interested in loud and showy experiences than silent contemplation. The original feeling of the wabi-sabi method can't be captured by imitation, but by inner contemplation felt by subconscious senses.

For those who lived in a period when materialism didn't exist, it was certainly easier to cultivate this connection with one's surroundings and inner self. Expecting to live with the old sense of wabi-sabi is almost impossible. Today, the most we can do is to separate a little time of our lives when we practice a little bit of this profound mind-calming, introspective experience.

We can't deny the reality surrounding us, but we can introduce habits and practices into our lives that reduce the negative effects of the 21st century, such as stress, superficiality, and overconsumption.

If I can criticize the wabi-sabi method in any manner, I would just say it is extra challenging to relate to it as a non-Japanese person who lives in the middle of the consumerist Zeitgeist. Failing to adopt this concept may cause frustration, loss of self- esteem, or the false belief that one is not disciplined enough.

Don't fall in these traps. Remember the essence of wabi-sabi: nothing is perfect, but that's perfectly fine. Therefore, if you feel that you adopted wabi-sabi in an imperfect way, you actually did the right thing.

CHAPTER 2: THE NORDIC WAY OF ORGANIZED LIVING

History and Heritage

When I'm talking about the "Nordics," I'm referring to the northern part of Europe. Historically, the countries representing Scandinavia or the Nordics are Norway, Sweden, Finland, Denmark, and Iceland. These countries bloom in a minimalist life and décor style, just like Japan, but in a completely different way. To understand the Nordic way of minimalism, I will talk a bit about the history of this exciting area of Europe.

The most widely known historical period of the Northern European countries is the Viking Age. Thank you, Hollywood. The Viking Age experienced its peak between 793 and 1066

CE. The date of their rising is commonly considered to be 793 CE, when Viking raiders occupied an important island monastery in England, Lindisfarne. The end of the Viking Age occurred around 1066 when the Norwegian king, Harald III., was defeated by the Saxon King, Harold Godwinson, at the Battle of Stamford Bridge.[xiii]

The ancestors of today's Scandinavians were fierce warriors with a strong spirit of exploration. The society was male-dominated, but as an interesting fact, women in the Viking Scandinavia did have an unusual degree of freedom, compared to other countries in Europe, or in Japan at that time. They could request a divorce and reclaim their dowry if their marriages ended. They could also own land, and if their husband died in battle, they could keep what their husbands had left, often becoming rich widows.[xiv]

The Nordic area's history during the centuries following the Viking Age was just as hectic and war-packed as of other European countries. They went through a forced Christianization (in opposition to their polytheist Norse religion, with strong emphasis on battle and honor focused on getting to Valhalla, a mythical heaven for fallen warriors). Between 1100 and 1600 CE, they tried to unify the region, but because of internal power struggles, this endeavor failed. In the 16th century, they (almost) uniformly undertook Lutheranism as religion. Starting from the 17th century until the end of World War II, a series of wars affected the region, including the Thirty Years' War (1618-1648), the Great Northern War (1700-1721), the Napoleonic Wars (1801-1814) and the two World Wars.[xv]

However, the region overcame all its difficulties and has emerged as the greatest collection of welfare states in Europe, with some of the highest GDPs of the continent and the world. How was this possible for Scandinavian countries that don't excel proportionately to their success in any natural resources? (The exception to this is Norway and their oil exports, and the others in ice.) When entire nations prevail under hostile circumstances, the answers lie in the living spirits, not in the inanimate values.

This is why I chose to examine deeper what we can learn from Scandinavians about survival and life improvement. I will seek answers on how to improve individual life to the extent of creating a happy welfare society.

Did you know?

Denmark is called the happiest country in the world. Sweden has one of the highest tax rates in the world with 51.4% of GDP, and yet people are generally happy to pay a high tax rate because of the social benefit returns (fun fact: the Swedish word for tax is "skatt," which means "treasure"). Did you know that Norway once knighted a penguin, or that Denmark, Finland, and Sweden were the three least corrupt countries in 2016?

My overall impression of the Scandinavians is that they certainly do something differently than most of us. I have a Swedish friend who is one of the most vivacious, vibrant, and motivated people I know. We went for a four-day trip to Norway to climb up to Trolltunga peak (you should Google this place, it is a bucket list spot). Every adventure has its ups and downs, especially for a beginner backpacker like me. After the second day, my Maslow pyramid was seriously damaged. I longed for normal food, better sleep, and an actual restroom where I wouldn't freeze my butt off — literally.

I was full of anger and desperation, while my Swedish friend was Buddha on Earth next to me. He was collected, totally in control of his misery (even though he traded his super-warm sleeping bag with my used and thin Australian one, so he was probably colder than me), and weirdly happy. He enjoyed the amazing view, appreciated the moment, and what's more, he *lived* in the moment. To me, that trip was a good lesson, and I learned a lot about myself, but even more about something that Swedish people call *lagom*.

What is Lagom, and How Can You Use it to Improve Your Life?

As I have seen in the press and on social media, *lagom* was the *hygge* of 2017. For those who are not familiar with the meaning of hygge, it is a Danish way of living well. Even though it doesn't have a direct translation to English, the closest concepts of it are coziness and the mental state of well-being. I will talk about hygge in more detail later. Right now, the only thing that matters about hygge is that over the past few years, there has been a great hype about it. Now, it seems that the hype has started to turn its face toward *lagom*, the Swedish hygge.

However, comparing the two concepts doesn't do justice to either of them. Somewhere behind the media hysteria, there are great and very applicable life-improving habits in these lifestyles that I experienced firsthand. They are not the Norwegian patterned, $30 wool socks on the internet. That is the part I think is pretty useless, and only brings more clutter and consumption into our lives.

By definition, *lagom* means "not too much, not too little — just the right amount." It is "adequate," "enough," "sufficient." Some folktales date the origins of lagom back to the Viking Age, being a contraction of the Viking phrase "laget om" (around the team). Vikings used to pass a horn filled with mead around in order for everybody to receive their fair share. *Laget om* was the phrase that specified the portion of mead for everybody. Broadly speaking, the word means consensus and equality.

Today, lagom can be connected to the idiom "less is more," and stands as a good alternative to the hoarding generated by consumerism.

"Back in the Viking days, mead would be passed around, laget om, and everyone would take their sips. Lagom today is not that different to that: There is something for everyone, if everyone just takes a lagom amount from the mead when it comes around," said Bronte Aurel, a Londoner Scandinavian Kitchen owner, to *Telegraph UK*.[xvi]

There is a great truth in her words; if everybody would take just as much as needed, many problems wouldn't exist in the world. I don't want to go as far as famine and pollution. I want to keep this centered on our personal sphere.

The more we have, the more we fear we'd lose it all. The more we carry, the harder it becomes. I can illustrate this with a simple example: my backpack on that ominous hiking to Trolltunga. It was a three-day trip in the mountains. Water was provided by the fjords every half-mile or so — better water than any I'd drank in my life. I was not carrying a three-day water supply around, and my backpack still weighed 42 pounds (19 kgs). I carried everything in that pack. I mean it: sunscreen, wet wipes, five pair of socks, exchange shoes, shorts (I still don't know why), a swimsuit, a book, a map, my cellphone charger, mosquito repellent, shower gel, toothpaste and brush (not travel-sized), a complete First Aid kit, an extra selfie stick, body lotion, Daddy issues — everything. And that's not to mention the necessary musts, such as a sleeping bag, extra light. I didn't even carry the tent and the food!

Thinking back now, my packing was a complete disaster. However, back then, I didn't feel safe without these objects. "What if there are poisonous mosquitos? What if my skin gets dry from hostile winds? What if I fall off Trolltunga and need an extra selfie stick to record my fall?" What was I thinking, really?

Do you have weird hoarding habits and fear that without your gadgets, doomsday would surely fall upon you? Don't think about extraordinary circumstances like I did on my hike. We don't have to go far to identify such items in our lives. Cellphones, for example, are the ultimate gadget we'd never part with. Some would react less harshly at losing their arms than they would at losing their smart phone. Have you seen people who have lost their phones? First, their face shows profound dismay, their eyes get fixated on one place, and their hands start hitting each pocket of their clothes as if they're trying to win a whack-a-mole game. In the meantime, their brain works faster than Ford's conveyor belt, processing the last occasions they used their phones. When they become aware that they put it in their left pocket, which now is empty, they start trembling with fear, mumbling "ph-ph-phone," and they collapse helplessly.

I don't want to make fun of them — I lost my phone once, and another time, it was stolen. There's nothing funny about it. Still, it's a replaceable object. "But my entire life was on that phone," some might protest. Isn't this insane? A phone is an important object in our lives, but truly believing that our life depends on it is too much. This is not lagom, in other words.

The lagom attitude toward this event would be to acknowledge the loss, think about how it can be prevented the next time, and then move on. Take action to replace the device. If the information on it is indeed crucial, take safety precautions in case you lose your phone. Save your data to Dropbox, iCloud, or make a backup of the data on your computer. There are many measures you can take to live your life more relaxed, and to protect yourself from unpredictable stressors.

How to handle cellphone loss is just one example of how can you use lagom thinking to your benefit. Lagom shows you how to be frugal, fair, and to create balance in every area of your life.

"Lagom is an overarching concept behind your life in general. Rather than fitting a bit of lagom into your day, it's more about your approach to your life as a whole," said Elliot Stocks, the co-editor and creative director of Bristol-based magazine *Lagom*.

During my research about lagom, I interviewed a few Swedish people, including my friend, to talk about lagom and what it means to them. They almost uniformly defined it as "not too much, not too little, just the right amount."

When I asked them about how this defines their lives, they were hesitant. To them, lagom is not a life-improvement goal, but the natural way of living life. They are thought to be in this "the right amount" mentality.

"Yes, every day, everyone does it. Not like we say it every day, but if I say I want lagom milk in the coffee, for example, people get it," said Seb from Malmö when I asked him if he could feel the presence of lagom in his daily life.

He explained to me that living life in lagom is not always conscious in Sweden. They just know. "We don't want it all big as most Americans do, let's say. We just want lagom," he added.

"Asking a Swede about lagom is like asking a bird about flying," Frederik, an engineer from Stockholm, said. "Living in moderation is part of our way of life. It applies to good and bad things equally. Each of us has an inner Gollum who warns us when we become too cocky, and boosts us if we become too shy. It's like keeping the personality in balance. But lagom doesn't moderate inner virtues only. We don't like to build the biggest house and flash our wealth. But we don't want to seem or be poor, either. Living in the middle ground and valuing equality perhaps roots in being a socialist country for generations."

"We keep balance in our working hours, in our fashion, the slices of cake we eat, even in how much milk we put in our coffee," said Helga, a student at Uppsala University.

"Contentment is not something we feel when having lots of things. Rather, a beautiful tree, a smile on your child's face, small everyday life things evoke it."

Lagom lifestyle lacks fussiness, has no demand for pretentiousness, and people live pleasantly in modest confidence. The surroundings are functional. Practical architecture and design, wholesomeness, and simple, healthy cuisine are the main external features of the Swedish lagom.

People think in a community level and not on the individual. It is a typical Scandinavian way of thinking. The social welfare focus certainly plays a role in strengthening the community-centric approach, but the real reason is something else.

These countries geographically are situated in the north side of the Northern Hemisphere. Although the countries are big, the population density is low. From ancient times, people have depended on each other.

Everybody had their role in the community, and others were counting on the roles to be fulfilled. Otherwise, the existence of the entire tribe was in danger. The hostile environment forced Scandinavians to depend on each other, to pay attention to each other, because individually, their chances of survival were diminished.

Today, the situation is not as drastic. However, the mentality is still the same. They strive for community wellbeing because that will bring fulfillment to the individual as well.

Swedes say that the first step to acquiring empirical lagom knowledge is to think more about the group than the individual. If the group benefits, the individual also benefits.

Lagom doesn't want you to be stuck in mediocrity, or never aim higher. It shows that obsessive excess and always thinking about what you don't have will doom you to live a sad life. You can aim for the same goals with a switch in your focus: look at what you have now, be grateful for it, and spend time with your loved ones. Keep the balance.

Lagom also puts a big emphasis on sustainability. Swedes are environmentally conscious. Everything that is used wastefully burdens Nature. You can't eat two big lunches at noon, and you can't wear two trousers at the same time. Swedish fashion brands, starting with Gudrun Sjödén in the 70s, were pioneers in eco fashion popularization. H&M constantly has an eco fashion line in their collections.

Today, we often feel pressure to aim for more, to seek the next big thing. Lagom encourages us to have balance in our lives, and to live simple.

Instead of stacking stuff, try stacking good habits. For example, while you brush your teeth, say thank you for everything you have. Or while going to work, plan out how you will make your friends and family smile today. Improve your own quality of life and the lives of those around you. Moderation doesn't mean you have to live a linear, boring life. It rather means that you, for your own sake, exclude everything from your life that can cause stress and unhappiness.

It is not excessive to go out for a snack and coffee once or twice a day to break free from work and socialize with colleagues. Swedes call the ritual of a snack and coffee "fika." Fika helps the Swedes not work longer than they should. It is much more than snack time. It is disconnecting for a few minutes and savoring the moment.

Remember the Japanese wabi-sabi? Fika is the Swedish way of practicing it, involving their senses during those brief moments of disconnection: the smell of freshly roasted coffee, the practical, rustic Swedish furniture, the delicious taste of a pastry, the chattering around them, and the warm embrace of a friend all add new energy and positive vibes to the rest of the day.

An American friend of mine asked me while I was enthusiastically telling him about lagom, "But within this philosophy, where's the incentive to work harder and grow for the better? What if others don't care about the group?"

The question is legitimate and totally worth pondering.

Focusing on group benefits makes sense in a country where everybody is likeminded, but what about a country where everybody seeks their personal wellbeing? If only one person considers group wellbeing and everyone else fights solo, there won't be breakthrough changes. Unless you want to move to a Scandinavian country where taxes are high, but social returns are equally high, and everybody accepts the importance of society fairness, positioning group benefits in front of your own won't work out so well.

As I said previously in this book, when you choose to adopt a nation's best habits, take them with a grain of salt. Use those parts that can benefit you in your own environment.

In our world, it makes more sense to bring out the most of your individual life and be happy. And if everybody strives to accomplish this goal, we'll be happier as a community. When I say "bring out the most," I don't mean that you should be boastful, or hoard valueless, expensive stuff. Bringing out the most of yourself means achieving self-contentment, having good relationships, and living the life you truly wish for. These wishes can perfectly fit into lagom mentality. "The right amount" can guide your life as an individual anywhere, anytime. It is a form of minimalism that keeps your spirit in perfect balance.

If you feel you have the right amount, you'll never be hungry and never feel too full. With lagom, you can't be poor or excessively rich, either. You may not be able to buy a whole diamond, but you'll always have something at the table.

If you feel you have enough, you won't feel stressed. The tricky part is to acknowledge when enough is enough. If you have enough, but can't be satisfied with it, that's when stress, discontent, and bitterness come into your life. Stress and worry won't give you more, and they won't move you forward. Physically, you'll be at the same place, but mentally, you'll sink deeper and deeper. Lagom is a good method to help you overcome these kinds of worries in your life.

Lagom's criticism

My criticism of lagom is that it can become a "frenemy" of the creative mind. It can help you overcome worries, but just as easily can take you into a place where you sink into a lukewarm comfort. Living life in a lagom way means that you blend in with the crowd and don't take risks. Creativity thrives when you face challenges, but lagom seems to aim to repress challenges in life. In a socialist welfare state, this can be good for everyday living, but in countries like the US, UK, and other non-socialist countries, it might become an obstacle rather than an aid to a good life.

How should the non-socialists use lagom? The answer to this question might be hidden in the word lagom itself — with moderation. As Oscar Wilde said, "Everything with moderation. Especially moderation." I think that the philosophy has quite a few very good and applicable points to improve your everyday life.

The secret is not to start acting like a plum when you're an apple. In other words, don't let the philosophy influence more of your life than is healthy. How can you know when it is *enough*? Whenever you start feeling stressed, bitter, or uncomfortable with your lagom life — then it is enough.

Key Takeaways from the Lagom Lifestyle:

- "Not too much, not too little — the right amount."

- The more you have, the more anxious you'll become about losing it. Help yourself by not hoarding more than you feel comfortable and calm with.

- "Don't try to occupy two chairs with one butt" (Hungarian proverb). In other words, pay attention to sustainability and don't take more than you need.

- Lagom lifestyle lacks fussiness and has no demand for pretentiousness.

- Keep your surroundings functional, rather than fancy.

- Instead of stacking stuff, try stacking good habits.

- Break free from work for 10 to 15 minutes and practice being in the moment. Meditate introspectively or socialize with others.

- If you feel you have enough, you won't feel stressed.

- Lagom is a way of appreciating what you have today, instead of stressing about the possible benefits of tomorrow.

How to Improve Your Everyday Life with Hygge

Hygge is a form of old-world Danish minimalist thinking. The word hygge (pronounced "hou-gah") roughly means an enhanced state of coziness. However, in practice, it is much more than that. In short, it means creating a warm atmosphere while enjoying the good things in life with the people you love. A cinnamon-scented candle is hygge. The fragrance of freshly cut firewood is hygge. Spending time with your family is hygge too. The most hygge moments are when sitting around a table, surrounded by candlelight, fire dancing in the fireplace, eating good food, and discussing with the people who are dearest to you the big questions in life.

Hygge is a little bit like love. You know it when you feel it, but you can't put into precise words what you mean.

"Hygge is about enjoying life's simple, cozy moments. It's like the minimalist concept just taken up a notch," is the definition given by Pia Edberg, the author of *The Cozy Life*. She tells a story in her book of how she got rid of most of her belongings after a personal crisis, trying to embrace minimalism and keeping only the functional. However, after a short while, she started missing those nice, cozy items that gave her small flat a personal touch.[xvii]

A minimalist lifestyle and hygge can coexist and bring better results if combined constructively. You don't have to invade your house with Norwegian-patterned quilts, cashmere pillows, and 10 pairs of wool socks. You can experience hygge without the stuff by drinking a delicious hot chocolate with your loved ones, or sipping white tea while reading a book in front of the window.

Hygge is most commonly related to home activities, such as homemade meals — especially during the winter holiday season.

But you can experience hygge in a café, or in a green field in summer sunshine too. Just be aware of the good moment — whether it is special or a simple spark of joy.

How and Why Did the "Hygge Culture" Develop?

Scandinavian counties have long, cold, dark winters. This is why some habits and the mindset related to coziness are winter-related. Generally, hygge is seasonless, and you can practice it anytime, anywhere. The Danes believe that the most hygge moments need a bit of darkness and cold. This way the fireplace, candlelight, and warm drinks are much more appreciated. Cold makes people get closer to warm up together.

Hygge plays a great role in Scandinavians being the happiest people in the world, even though they live in darkness most of the time. We can say that developing a method that makes the depressing environment bearable was a survival technique.

Since Christmas is a celebration of love and people usually spend it with their families, it's not surprising that it became the most hygge time of the year.

Hygge is strongly connected with the feeling of safety as well. You can sense hygge in places where you feel protected, safe, and happy. In most of the cases, this place is what you consider home. If you want to adopt the hygge lifestyle, it is important to give and keep your home in a shape that inspires you, makes you happy and calm to spend time in, and ultimately gives you a feeling of safety.

Hygge can make you healthier, happier, and more creative.

Why?

Because you connect the cozy feeling of your favorite blanket or book, or your spouse's smile, to safety. Your brain maps these associations, and every time you think about these things, the brain will trigger dopamine, oxytocin, and other hormones responsible for happiness. If you think or experience hygge, the executive part of the brain gets activated in the cortex. You'll feel mentally and physically safe and your guard won't be up — you'll have the capacity to think creatively, to learn easier, and to stress less.

How Can You Activate the Hygge Button in Your Life?

Some compare hygge to the Japanese way of mindfulness and meditation. Even if the mindfulness part is true, while the Japanese sense of meditation requires silent introspection, mostly in solitude, hygge is quite the opposite. Hygge is a mindful, meditative state you actively share with others. You let the world in, instead of trying to lock it out.

However, we are not all the same. Some may experience hygge best by being alone, quietly sipping a mug of cocoa, reading *Pride and Prejudice*, or watching the rain. Hygge doesn't really have rules. You have to feel it in your heart, and just like with love, you'll know when you're in a hygge mood.

Hygge is not a constructed reality. It is not like you go on the street and some things are hygge and some are not. Hygge comes from within, and therefore, every situation, every place, and every moment can have some hygge — you just have to find it. Ultimately, it's a feeling you filter through your own heart. If you don't want to feel it, you can be in the coziest gingerbread house and nothing special will happen. If your heart is ready to accept hygge, you'll be able to find it on the street, on a rainy day, in the soaked, colorful leaves and in the little bubbles big raindrops leave in the mud, and in a street cat patiently resting in an overturned bucket, waiting for drier times.

Enjoy the moments for what they are and not what you want them to be. Hygge can't be manufactured. Just seek out the good in things, spend quality time with your loved ones as much as possible, and on a casual Tuesday evening it will hit you, and you know this is the feeling.

How to Bring Hygge Into Your Environment

Although cozy things don't necessarily make you feel hygge, clutter and chaos will surely prevent you from feeling it. Clutter always comes with stress, anxiety, and a lot of dust.

Decluttering in hygge terms doesn't mean to throw out most of your stuff and keep only 10 items per room. It means keeping only the things that are essential (functional) and add value to your life (emotional, mental, or spiritual). In some regards, the approach is not too different from the KonMari method. Keep the useful things and those which spark joy. However, the KonMari method takes item selection more seriously than the hygge.

Hygge is all about coziness, calmness, and happiness. Clutter and dust can evoke stress hormones, restlessness, and discomfort, which is everything hygge is not. This is why you can't escape decluttering if you want to adopt a hygge lifestyle. After decluttering, you'll feel less stressed. The less mess you have around you, the freer and more in control you'll feel.

Danish, and generally Scandinavian, houses have white walls. It is timeless, elegant, expands the perception of space, and makes the house brighter. They use earth-colored furnishings and decorations such as ceiling beams, drawers, chairs, couches, and wooden floors. Most Scandinavian houses have at least one fireplace. Scandinavians use white, cream, brown, black, navy blue, and similar shades for home décor.

Hygge decorations inevitably include some candles and family pictures on the walls. Soft textures are also hygge. Fluffy carpets, wooly rugs, quilts, and pillows can add an extra touch of coziness. Cashmere, faux fur, and merino wool are all warm and inviting. The oft-mentioned Norwegian pattern design can inspire that Christmas-like coziness.

Alternatively, you can have some green plants or herbs in your windows or in other spots in the house. Living things, like flowers, always add life and vibrancy to the space. Herbs such as mint, lavender, or basil have amazing natural scents that can help you relax even more. Mint and basil are refreshing scents which help you to focus. Lavender is especially helpful before sleeping. It has a calming, relaxing aroma.

The Hygge Cuisine

Since hygge is all about coziness and heartwarming feelings, the food related to it is initially what you like the most.

In Danish culture, hygge meals are mostly homemade and usually are winter-connected. Hot chocolate, different kinds of pastries, and baked apples with cinnamon are all hygge, but also healthy, low-carb meals rich in green vegetables can be hygge.

Some special hygge meals are chicken soup with herbs and root vegetables, fish soups, grilled vegetables, and salmon. My personal favorite, however, is a dessert recipe called lemon mousse. I will share the secret with you here. It has a refreshing citrus flavor that makes it a good choice in both the summer and winter. Since I only savored this delicacy in Copenhagen, I asked for help from *The Guardian* newspaper in providing you with this authentic recipe. The following recipe is from the article, "Hungry for Hygge: Trine Hahnemann's Scandi Comfort Food."

> For 6-8 servings you need the following ingredients:

- gelatin 6 sheets, 9 g in total (0.3 oz)
- eggs 6, separated
- caster sugar 150 g (5.3 oz)
- double cream 400 ml (1.7 cups)
- lemon juice 150 ml (0.6 cups)

- grated zest of unwaxed lemon 1

To serve:
- whipping cream 200 ml (0.85 cups), whipped
- unwaxed lemon zest 1 tbsp, julienned

"Soak the gelatin in cold water for about 5 minutes. Beat the egg yolks and sugar together with an electric mixer until pale and fluffy.

In another clean bowl, whisk the egg whites until fluffy. In a third bowl, whip the cream until light and fluffy. Drain the gelatin and place in a small pan to melt. When melted, take off the heat and add the lemon juice and zest. Slowly add the lemon and gelatin mixture to the egg yolk mixture, carefully stirring all the time. Now fold in the egg whites and the whipped cream.

Pour into 6 serving glasses and put the rest of the mixture into a big serving bowl for second helpings. Chill in the fridge for a couple of hours or overnight before serving.

Serve with the whipped cream and julienned lemon zest on top. The mousse will keep in the fridge for 3-4 days."[xviii]

I hope you'll enjoy this refreshing dessert as much as I did. You'll be luckier if you have the experience in the comfort of your home. I had it at a small window service shop in 38-degree Fahrenheit weather. I didn't feel so hygge back then, to be honest, but it is still a lovely memory. I guess the memory became hygge after the event.

I must add that hygge food is not always about health. Danes have lots of bakeries and eat lots of pastries — especially on Friday. They call it *fredagsslik*. Even if candies and cookies are the delicious accessories of any good day, maybe this hygge habit shouldn't be in the top five you decide to apply to your life. At least, not every Friday. Choose one Friday a month that you dedicate to Godiva.

My Personal Hygge Experience

I visited Denmark in March 2016. It was a brief visit of five days. Back then, I still had a job and I couldn't take more days off. Denmark in March is still very cold, and occasionally rainy.

What I first noticed was that people seemed very sporty. Many were outside jogging on the almost frozen roads, and even more were on bicycles. My boyfriend and I were wearing three layers of warm clothes, shivering while the Scandies ran around in sweatshirts and thin jackets. One day, when it was 10 degrees Celsius (50 degrees Fahrenheit) outside, in the middle of summertime, they cheerfully walked around in flip-flops. They didn't look gloomy or depressed at all. Everybody looked as if life was a laid-back condition; there was no rush in the world, and the concept of cold didn't exist in their dictionary.

I wouldn't consider them particularly friendly or rude people, either. They were normal and let us, obvious tourists (scarves, down jackets, closed-toe shoes), be. I felt a strange feeling of calmness when we were there.

We stayed at an Airbnb place. It was the ultimate hygge house with a very comfortable bed, wooden furnishings, quilts everywhere, and an old vinyl player in the corner with some records.

Copenhagen is a charming little city. Even if the sky was gray, everything around was colorful and cheerful. Danes may keep their interior design simple, but they are not shy with their exterior color choices. Every building was vibrant — red, purple, blue, green, yellow, and other bright shades were used. The cityscape looked like those pictures where you Photoshop the sky black and white, but leave the rest in full color. Cold, but cozy.

Overall, I enjoyed our Denmark trip a lot. We could find our own way of feeling hygge, curling up together in the furry blankets on the sofa while sipping warm tea and listening to Sinatra on the record player.

The Criticism of Hygge

Trying to always live on the cozy side may take us to a weird mixture of La Land and Hobbiton. If embracing coziness is used to have a safe haven where we can retire after a long and exhausting day, that's okay. If we want to replace reality, forget about our credit card balance, and hide our heads in the sand with coziness, it is not okay. Just like I said about lagom, hygge also needs moderation. Truly special moments fade in the pits of routine if we experience them too often.

Denmark and other Scandinavian countries, like Norway and Sweden, are constantly selected among the happiest nations in the world. Denmark scored the title of "The Best" in 2012, 2013, and 2016. This may be partially in thanks to hygge. There are other statistics about the Scandies that are not as popular and well-known.

Did you know?

According to a report of the OECD countries, Iceland leads the world in antidepressant consumption with 101 daily doses per 1,000 people, tightly followed by Denmark, Sweden, and Finland. These kinds of medications and drugs are easily accessible to citizens in Scandinavian countries. Another report showed that almost 40% of Danish women and 32% percent of Danish men receive mental health treatment at some point during their lives.

Researchers proved that Finns and Danes are the top two candy and sugar confectionery eaters of the world. This phenomena is entwined with the concept of hygge. Eating a bowlful of candy is totally normal in Hyggeland. Fredagsslik (Friday Candy Time) is a ritual. It is practiced in family homes nationwide. In 2002, the FAO (Food and Agriculture Organization) published a report showing Denmark had the highest meat consumption per capita in the world (145.9 kg/322 lbs). In 2009, these numbers changed to a milder set (95.3 kg/210 lbs) which "was enough" to qualify them for 13th place instead.

"It is almost required to eat unhealthily when you hygge," a friend of mine who currently lives in Denmark told me. She also told me that Danes take hygge to an almost coercive level. If someone (mostly expats) doesn't practice hygge by their rules, the whole cozy get-together can turn into an ugly exclusion of foreigners who bring religion, politics, or other non-hygge topics to the table. Generally speaking, Danes are not a very foreigner-friendly country. In 2016, they scored the 50th place out of 67, according to a survey by *Expat Insider*.

This data don't mean that Danes or Scandinavians in general are rude and depressed, but the reports of them being the happiest people in the world should be taken with a pinch of salt.

There are many aspects of hygge lifestyle that are worth giving a try. Maybe it will be life-changing for you.

Key Takeaways from Hygge Mentality:

- Spend more time with your family and friends.

- Create special moments for yourself, even when there's nothing special around, by recalling previous moments of coziness.

- Connect the small moments of happiness with safety.

- Try to cook more at home and savor it.

- Declutter to be less stressed. Keep your functional items and combine them with cozy ones.

- Use natural colors and comfortable materials to decorate your home.

BECOME THE MASTER OF YOUR SPACE

I presented four significant and unique interpretations of minimalism that can lead to a good life. While all of them make complete sense in their home country, and people sometimes practice them unconsciously, they might not be so easily applicable in your life.

If you're a more extroverted, cheerful, and loud person, the silent, contemplative wabi-sabi method might be very hard to practice. Or if you're Australian, you might not understand what's so cozy and magical in winter, since in your hemisphere, Christmas is celebrated on the beach in bikinis. This is why I said in the beginning that your success at making order in your life does not depend on how much you adopt a minimalist method. It depends on how well you use the one or two methods, and the advice you choose to follow.

Maybe you wish for cozy home décor, clothes flawlessly folded, and to not live in excess — to have just the right amount of everything. Then check out hygge for decorations, fold your things like Marie Kondo, and read more about lagom and practice control in your everyday life.

The information I shared in this book is enough for you to decide which path to head down, if any of the presented methods sound good to you. If you choose to follow some of the tips, you'll be able to downsize and minimalize your environment, and maximize the comfort of your home and life in general. However, if you want to dig deeper and gather more knowledge about any of the four methods, I strongly recommend you to read the references I mention at the end of this book.

Minimalism comes from within. At the end of the day, you are the only one who can know how many things you feel comfortable living with. I can't tell you in a book that if you don't throw out this or that, you'll be doomed to eternal unhappiness. That's stupid. What I can do is to show you as many alternatives as possible about how to start, execute, and maintain that life change you're seeking. I know you want some clutter-freeness, otherwise you wouldn't have bought this book.

At the end of the day, decluttering is not the hardest part. Preventing re-cluttering is hard. This is why I believe in philosophies that help us decide to make a daily routine change in our lives. Momentary passion is not enough to maintain long-term results. This is why adopting a little bit of the wabi-sabi mentality or lagom lifestyle can help you stay on track and not fall back to clutter. Remind yourself that imperfect is beautiful, and excess won't make you happy.

Last year, I gave away most of my things, and I told the story and my methods in *Less Mess Less Stress*. Two years have passed, and I still have only a luggage bag full of things with which I travel. I follow two simple rules, thanks to which I can keep maintaining this level of minimalism. These rules can be applied in any situation.

My first rule is that if I buy something, I throw something out in return. This usually is not difficult to execute because I only buy new things if something gets trashed. For instance, last week, I bought a new pair of running shoes because my pinky toe had too much freedom, and I feared it might escape through the hole of the previous set. It was very difficult to let those shoes go, though. They were a pair of 12-year-old Adidases that I got from my mom (I got very few things from my mom). As I learned in the KonMari method, I thanked the shoes for their long, faithful service. I packed them into the box from the new shoes (like a coffin) and put them in the trashcan.

If the reason for a new purchase is not necessity, but simple desire, that's okay too. However, if you aim to keep your house clutter-free, you have to be tough and throw something out to make space for the new item. Keeping this drastic measure in mind while shopping can prevent you from making useless purchases.

My second rule for keeping myself clutter-free is a mind game. I imagine that I buy the item, some months or years pass, and a fire breaks out in my home. I ask myself two questions related to this scenario: Would this item be among those very few that I'd try to save from the fire? (I'd probably save my computer.) If I let this item burn in the fire, would it be among those very few that I would feel truly sorry about losing? (Definitely my computer.)

If my honest answer is "no" for both questions, I simply walk away and don't buy it. If I give the answer "yes" to either of these questions, I seriously ponder about buying the item. However, even if I'm keen on buying it, it still has to pass through the first rule. If I can't find anything that I can throw out to make space for this new item, I usually don't buy it. It sounds harsh, but discipline is not easy. It's my personal interpretation of minimalism in my current stage life — I want it to fit into my luggage.

You don't have to be so hard on yourself. Know your goals and act, declutter, and minimize accordingly.

Remember, books just give you tips and directions. You have the power and freedom to apply them — what you wish, as much as you wish, and for as long as you wish. The only aim here is to make yourself as happy as possible.

I believe in you. It's time to create your own imperfectly perfect, cozy, minimal, good enough universe.

Yours truly,
Zoe

Reference

Books:

Edberg, Pia. *The Cozy Life.* Self-published, 2016. E-book.

Ford, Arielle. *Wabi Sabi Love: The Ancient Art of Finding Perfect Love in Imperfect Relationships*. Harper Elixir. 2013.

Hesmyr, Atle. *Scandinavia in the Early Modern Era; From Peasant Revolts and Witch Hunts to Constitution Drafting Yeomen*. Nisus Publications. 2015.

Ikeno, Osamu, & Davies, Roger. *The Japanese Mind*. Japan: Tuttle Publishing, 2002. E-book.

Kendrick, T.D. *A History of the Vikings*. Dover Publications. 2004.

Kondo, Marie. *The Life Changing Magic of Tiding Up.* Berkeley: Ten Speed Press, 2014. E-book.

Lawrence, Robyn Griggs. *Simply Imperfect: Revisiting the Wabi-Sabi House.* New Society Publishers. 2011.

Web pages:

InterNations. Expat Insider 2016: Three Years of Insights. 2016.
https://www.internations.org/expat-insider/

The Economist. Moreover: Very clean people, the Japanese. 1997.
http://www.economist.com/node/153179

The Guardian. World: Europe: Hygge — why the craze for Danish cosiness is based on a myth. 2016.
https://www.theguardian.com/world/shortcuts/2016/sep/04/hygge-denmark-

danes-cosiness-wealth-antidepressants-scandinavians

The Guardian. Lifestyle: Food and Drink: Hungry for hygge: Trine Hahnemann's Scandi comfort food.
https://www.theguardian.com/lifeandstyle/2016/oct/23/hungry-for-hygge-trine-hahnemanns-scandi-comfort-food

The Telegraph. Lifestyle: Wellbeing: Mood and Mind. Hart, Anna. Goodbye Hygge, hello Lagom: the secret of Swedish contentment. 2017.
http://www.telegraph.co.uk/wellbeing/mood-and-mind/goodbye-hygge-hello-lagom-secret-swedish-contentment/

Endnotes

[i] DeAngelis, Tori. *Consumerism and its discontents*. American Psychology Association. 2004.
http://www.apa.org/monitor/jun04/discontents.aspx
[ii] DeAngelis, Tori. *Consumerism and its discontents*. American Psychology Association. 2004.
http://www.apa.org/monitor/jun04/discontents.aspx
[iii] DeAngelis, Tori. *Consumerism and its discontents*. American Psychology Association. 2004.
http://www.apa.org/monitor/jun04/discontents.aspx
[iv] Statista. *Total number of hot springs (onsen) in Japan from 2005 to 2014 (in thousands)*. Statista. 2018.
https://www.statista.com/statistics/682636/japan-hot-spring-numbers/
[v] Ikeno, Osamu, & Davies, Roger. *The Japanese Mind*. Japan: Tuttle Publishing, 2002. E-book.
[vi] Ikeno, Osamu, & Davies, Roger. *The Japanese Mind*. Japan: Tuttle Publishing, 2002. E-book.

[vii] Kondo, Marie. *The Life Changing Magic of Tiding Up.* Berkeley: Ten Speed Press, 2014. E-book.

[viii] Ikeno, Osamu, & Davies, Roger. *The Japanese Mind.* Japan: Tuttle Publishing, 2002. E-book.

[ix] Ikeno, Osamu, & Davies, Roger. *The Japanese Mind.* Japan: Tuttle Publishing, 2002. E-book.

[x] Ikeno, Osamu, & Davies, Roger. *The Japanese Mind.* Fukumoto, 1983, pp. 10—11. Japan: Tuttle Publishing. 2002. E-book.

[xi] Lawrence, Robyn Griggs. *Simply Imperfect: Revisiting the Wabi-Sabi House.* New Society Publishers. 2011.

[xii] Ford, Arielle. *Wabi Sabi Love: The Ancient Art of Finding Perfect Love in Imperfect Relationships.* Harper Elixir. 2013.

[xiii] Kendrick, T.D. *A History of the Vikings.* Dover Publications. 2004.

[xiv] Kendrick, T.D. *A History of the Vikings.* Dover Publications. 2004.

[xv] Hesmyr, Atle. *Scandinavia in the Early Modern Era; From Peasant Revolts and Witch Hunts to Constitution Drafting Yeomen.* Nisus Publications. 2015.

[xvi] Hart, Anna. *Goodbye Hygge, hello Lagom: the secret of Swedish contentment.* Telegraph. 2017. http://www.telegraph.co.uk/health-fitness/mind/goodbye-hygge-hello-lagom-secret-swedish-contentment/

[xvii] Edberg, Pia. *The Cozy Life.* Self-published, 2016. E-book.

[xviii] Hahnemann, Trine. *Hungry for hygge: Trine Hahnemann's Scandi comfort food.* The Guardian. 2016. https://www.theguardian.com/lifeandstyle/2016/oct/23/hungry-for-hygge-trine-hahnemanns-scandi-comfort-food